be steady, my soul

daily practices for peace and positivity

love collins

love collins

for God, Ollie, & Sandra

love collins

CONTENTS

"And he arose, and rebuked the wind, and said unto the sea, Peace, be still. And the wind ceased, and there was a great calm."

- Mark 4:39

1

Be Still

*"Be like a mountain in the wind.
Do you notice how it moves?"*
— Rumi, tr. by Coleman Barks

Blow, wind, blow. When the winds of adversity sweep your way and the rains of circumstance fill your ship, find quiet strength in stillness. You can remain unshaken by the ebb and flow of life and your own ever-changing emotions when you practice being motionless.

Consider how the mountain stays still in the storm. It is unmovable. At the same time it touches the ground it touches the sky. It experiences both highness and lowness at once. The snow, the sunshine, the outer circumstances never seem to disturb the mountain. Be like the mountain—be still.

Society doesn't honor stillness. It praises *busyness*. It pays productivity. Sadly, the need for constant movement rubs against your ability to be at peace. The friction eventually creates a fire, and most of us don't attempt to quell the flames until our entire house is ablaze. Just like the hour and minute hands on our watches, we run in circles. This is so dizzying.

Being busy comes from a misinterpretation of time. Time is not real. It's imaginary. It's just a measurement: distance divided by speed. We attempt to quantify it, even though the true nature of time is limitless. Limiting behavior is the result of limiting beliefs. You rush because you think the sand in the hourglass is always about to expire. When you stop seeing time as scarce and start seeing it as abundant, you are then free to be still. Stillness allows you to experience peace.

Challenge

Sit down. Rise up straight in your seat. Become aware of the cushion and the legs supporting you. Breathe in ten, long, lung-filling breaths. Gaze forward unbothered, watching time pass. Inhaling, think everything. Exhaling, think nothing.

When I started practicing stillness periods, I would try not to move for ten minutes, then fifteen, then twenty. Sitting there and doing nothing felt so bizarre. My mind traveled miles. My nose itched. I had to scratch it. I was having *busy-ness* withdrawals. Finally, my mind settled. My body grew distant. The thoughts became less frequent.

Your brain thinks tens of thousands of

thoughts every day—some experts say 50,000. That's upwards of 35 thoughts per minute. The mind must be trained to be still. Even sleep is not enough to tame it. Think about dreams. During your semi-conscious state, your mind keeps moving, creating pictures and mental movies.

Stillness periods and moments of meditation tranquilize the wild beast of thought. Your thoughts, in turn, become more clear and creative. You can finally focus. You can tap into the wisdom that mountains speak of: the wisdom of stillness.

Soul Talk

Relax. There's no rush.
The world can wait. I am no longer a slave
to busy-ness like everyone else.
I choose to enjoy this breath.
I choose to be timeless, to be still, to be free.

2

The Rehearsal

*It happened. Don't let it happen a thousand
more times by rehearsing it in your mind.*

— love collins

The past is dead. The failures and mistakes of yesterday are buried in the tomb of time. When you rehearse all the moments that have already been lived, you resurrect them. Without you the past is powerless. It has no strength to come back on its own.

So why is it so natural to rehearse what she said or what he did? Well, let's be real. A small piece of us finds comfort in the place of misery. It's lonely but warm there. It's dark yet safe. As the movie reel plays on repeat on the projector of your conscious, you convince yourself that your bad mood is justified. "You have a right to be angry," a voice whispers. "They should have never treated you that way." In the end, the grumbling only leaves you empty. Realize that thoughts of anger and frustration are not worthy of you.

The act of rehearsal is just your imagination working against you instead of in your favor like it's supposed to. The thing you are remembering is not happening at *this* moment; therefore, it is no longer real. What's real is your response: grudge or grace?

When it comes to our past, typically there is a much deeper matter to address. The root of constant rehearsal of the same old lines is an indication that there is someone in the past you need to forgive. Sometimes that someone who caused you pain is a person you love or look up to. Maybe they said something careless that cut you to the quick. Their negative words are now chiseled into your mind.

Accept the fact that people will have their opinions about you. Thankfully, however, their interpretation of you doesn't define your reality. You exist independently, outside of their opinions. The words they aim at you are just water guns. The lies they spray cannot penetrate the truth of who you are.

But sometimes the person you must forgive is you. Self-forgiveness can be the most challenging form of forgiveness. The voice is so familiar. "You should have known better. How could you do something so stupid?" We batter ourselves.

Embrace gentleness. It happened. Don't let it happen a thousand more times by rehearsing it in your mind. Just as a mother nurses the wound of her child, who by his own foolishness touched the hot stove, you too need the tender touch of forgiveness in order to heal. Remind yourself that this is your first attempt at life. You will make mistakes. You will slip into pitfalls that were clearly marked. You will take detours when the shorter, smoother route was right in front of you. This is the true trauma of being human.

There is no need to remind yourself that you were a *homo sapien* and failed. That has already been factored into the equation of your life. God knew you would fall. The measure of who you are, however, is not the number of times you stumble but the times you rise back up—so rise.

Challenge

If you must imagine the past, re-tell the story. Construct the best possible scenario, and tell yourself that this version is the real version. Notice how you are suddenly inspired to take action. Where it once was an anchor holding you down, your past becomes a sail.

Soul Talk

I forgive others like I forgive myself.
I forgive myself completely.

3

The Art of Exit

I'm no fool. I know when it's time to move on.
I find the exit sign when the welcome mat is gone.
— love collins

I magine you're at an elegant cocktail party. It's a black-tie event. You're dressed to the tens. Old friends are shaking hands and giving dap as they pour into the room. The server offers you a cube of cheese and white wine. Suddenly, someone runs from the kitchen yelling "fire!" People panic. Smoke rolls from under the doorway. What do you do?

You leave. You decide to do what any sane person would—get to the nearest exit. Even though this is the natural response to real fires, how come it's seldom a reflex to leave life situations when our peace is in flames? Too often we move in when it's really time to move on. We battle back and forth with ourselves about whether to leave or stay in a toxic relationship we know can only end in ruin for both sides. We remain at a job years past the expiration date. All the while, our inner sanctuary gets singed.

So why do we do it? Why remain in a place even when staying there runs counter to our solace and happiness? Fear. Mark the atlas of your life, and you will find that anytime you outstayed your welcome in a negative space, it was probably because you were just a little too scared to leave. You were afraid of burning a bridge or losing a friend or being lonely.

Deep down you knew the right move to make. Even today, there is a situation or relationship where the big, red EXIT sign is flashing. There is an art to making an exit. You have to know whether you really should stick it out and see what the end will be or make a run for it. Here are some signs: If it (whatever or whoever *it* is) brings you more stress than joy, exit. If it is not causing you to grow (mentally, financially, emotionally or spiritually), exit. If it is not affirming your true worth, exit. If it is taking too much and giving too little, proceed to the nearest exit.

For you to remain miserable in a smothering environment where you are neither permitted nor encouraged to become the best version of yourself is suicidal for your destiny. Eventually you will reach the breaking point, which won't be good for you or anyone else who is hit by the debris. What about when exiting is not an option? As a parent, you can't just abandon your child. As a student who has paid thousands of dollars for tuition, dropping out might not be practically or financially wise. As an employee or employer, leaving your business because you're upset could leave you with a stack of bills and more stress. Do a modified version of the Exit: the Be Right Back.

Challenge

When you catch your anger simmering and the pot of anxiety boiling over within you, take a mental health day or a mental health moment.

When and only when you have returned to yourself, come back. Your temporary pause will bring so much relief. Even though the house might still be in flames and the situation un-changed, at least you were able to leave and go get a water hose and put on a gas mask. Be your exit temporary or permanent, just getting out the door to where you can reclaim your peace is the ultimate goal.

Soul Talk

I'm no fool. I know when it's time to move on. I find the exit sign when the welcome mat is gone.

4

Be Grateful

"As we express our gratitude, we must never forget that the highest appreciation is not to utter words but to live by them."
— John F. Kennedy

What you are grateful for grows. The word gratitude comes from the Latin term *gratus* meaning pleasing or thankful. It's hard to entertain feelings of sadness and to be pleasantly full of gratitude at the same time. Verbalizing your state of appreciation instantly shifts your focus away from any perceived lack. Negative people and habitual complainers call themselves realist. They dismiss those who are positive as being naïve optimists. What they misunderstand, though, is the Law of Magnification. This law simply states that the longer you stare at an object the more of it you tend to notice.

Try this. Hold your pinky finger six inches in front of your nose. For eight seconds look directly at your finger. Study it. Notice the shape, the length of your nail, the dark crease lines. Now, with your finger still in place, look beyond it. Direct your attention to the space ahead of you. Your finger is still there, but it's just a blur and a minor obstruction to your wider view.

Gratitude works the same way. It's not an escape trick that makes your problems disappear; it simply shifts your focus. Gratitude lets you see the many blessings—food, clothing, water, family, friends—and blocks out the pinky problems you are facing.

Thinking about what you're grateful for is not half as effective as actually writing down a list of ten, twenty, or thirty reasons why you are grateful. I've kept a blue notepad beside my bed for months. When I wake up in the morning, I open it up to the second page and begin reading from the list of people, experiences, and talents God has allowed me to enjoy. I even give thanks for things I don't have yet. If I roll over in a frantic mood, I find the words: "I am grateful for peace of mind." Immediately, my thoughts huddle around images of tranquility like a football team before the snap. Act grateful even when you don't feel it.

Express gratitude for the country you want to travel to or that new vehicle you see yourself driving or even the soul mate you are expecting to enter your life. Possession begins first in the mind. As you express gratitude for your present gift of singleness, you can also welcome the gift of new relationships. Be thankful for it all, even the small stuff.

Challenge

Write someone you care about a handwritten note. Detail how grateful you are to have that person in your life.

What you are grateful for grows. The more thankful you are the more you find to be thankful for. People will gravitate toward you. The energy you exude will spread like a contagion, and all the situations you were complaining about will have dwarfed next to the abundance of joy and peace you attract.

Soul Talk

I am so grateful for all the phenomenal people, places, and experiences currently in my life as well as those that are now entering my life.

5

The Turtle's Shell

"You may not control all the events that happen to you,
but you can decide not to be reduced by them."

— Maya Angelou

I was talking to a family member the other day. I heard something in her throat. Was it tension or disappointment? I didn't know. I only knew I sensed the sound of pain suspended beneath the surface of our conversation. It turned out that her close friend, practically her sister, had nearly died the day before. The doctor discovered a blood clot that could have been fatal. My relative took it hard.

When you are the type of person who loves deeply and who emotionally connects with the struggles of others, the prick of their pain can pierce your skin. Because your compassion for them is so fierce, their circumstances almost feel like your reality. This is the essence of empathy. It is what makes you human. It can also be the source of much suffering. You were not made to suffer. Your body is specifically wired to react adversely to pain. Touch a hot kettle, your hand will jerk. Walk into a smoky room, you will start to cough. You are not meant for struggle. Nevertheless, when you hear of the difficulties those around you are enduring, it feels natural to identify with their situation. They are, of course, an extension of you. The same memories of them that live inside your mind manifest as memories of you inside of theirs. The connection is real.

Despite it all, you must liberate yourself from their pain. Your suffering does not add to their joy. Your distress does not enhance their peace. You were designed to be filled with love and happiness, not sadness. Even if the circumstances around you depict lack, you can abide in abundance. While others are caught in fear, you can remain in faith. They may be in extreme illness, but you can experience overwhelming health. Love them. Support them. Walk beside them. Do not, however, take ownership of their problems. Be free from that which does not nourish your soul.

Is this greedy? Is it selfish to protect yourself from the circumstances around you? A little. But remember, the turtle's shell is hard because its head is soft. You need protection too. You are to be the light that fills their darkness. If your bulb is dim with distress, how will anyone see? If you are in a state of strength and your neighbor is in a place of weakness, it serves neither of you to dwell in the sulking place together. Be the source of power from which they draw so both of you can thrive.

Upon deeper reflection, you may find that your pain is sometimes selfishness disguised as empathy. You don't want to lose that friend, do you? Where would you be without that loved one? Chances are your condition leads back to your own fear of future hurt. Shed that layer of selfishness and you will see that what they really need is for you to be their solid foundation. Or maybe you're the one in need of a shoulder to lean on. If not now, you will be. The greatest stumbling block to your recovery can be a well-meaning friend. After the initial act that harmed you has passed, you need someone strong next to you. This is not the time to be pampered or to commiserate. A true friend will tell you the unfriendly truth. "You can't stay in this place of weeping, and I won't stand here holding your tissue. Let's move past this. Let's grow."

Soul Talk

I am immune to the circumstances surrounding me. Yes, I do care deeply for the hurting, but I will not adopt their hurt. Rather, I will offer them the healing and happiness that overflows within me.

6

The Beauty in the Beast

*"Think of all the beauty still left around you
and be happy."*

— Anne Frank

Rub your eyes and see. Where is the beauty here in this person, this place, and this predicament? If you don't see the beauty within the beast that you are facing right now, chances are it's not because the beauty is not there but because you have not discovered it yet. To tell you the truth, sometimes the beauty won't even be outwardly visible. Some days you will meet with attitudes you can't stand and enter environments where you will see no external evidence of beauty, but non-visible does not mean non-existent. You don't have to see the wind to view which way it is blowing.

The difference is not *what* you're looking at but *how* you are looking at it. A leaf appears uninteresting until you put it under a microscope. The moon can seem unimpressive until grab a pair of binoculars. Perspective changes everything. Let's say your best friend is dating a jerk. You know it. Her mom knows. Her cousins know. Everybody sees him as a jerk except her. She sees his charm, his wit, his determined mindset and thinks he's flawless. The name for this is repression. She's directing all her attention toward his good qualities and subconsciously smothering the bad ones. What she sees is the beauty in the beast (for better or worse). You can do the same thing with any challenging circumstance.

Psychiatrist Viktor Frankl, a Holocaust survivor, explained how he uncovered hope in the most miserable situation in *Man's Search for Meaning.* "I told my comrades (who lay motionless, although occasionally a sign could be heard) that human life, under any circumstances, never ceases to have meaning." By finding beauty in suffering and even death, he was able to survive.

I'll never forget the start of my second year of law school. I checked my school account and saw that my scholarship had not been applied to my account. School was only a few days away and I was getting worried. I hurried to my computer and contacted the dean who helped me get the award in the first place. It was too late. I heard the words in his sigh before he even said them: "I'm sorry, but you've lost your scholarship." Those words stung. There I was days before classes with a huge bill and a shattered ego. After a moment of disappointment and self-pity, I shook myself and asked: "Where is the beauty?" There it was. I learned to appreciate the gift of getting a professional degree. I learned the beauty of having family members who loved me and were willing to give me a helping hand instead of kicking me to the ground in reprimand. I learned that having to pay more made me work harder and eventually get the highest GPA I had earned up to that semester. When you dig for the good in all circumstances, you notice that it's always right there, just below the surface. A seed is hidden in every struggle.

Challenge

Look for the beauty. If you are driving down the road and somebody cuts you off, there goes your opportunity to see the beauty of patience in the beast of haste. If you had big plans to go out with friends, but you get sick, there is your chance to see the beauty in stillness.

Soul Talk

There is beauty in this beast I am facing.
I may not see it, but I will find it.
As I embrace the good, all else will melt away.

7

Guard Your Heart

"Above all else, guard your heart,
for everything you do flows from it."
— Proverbs 4:3

We lock our car doors. We install alarm systems in our houses. We even put passcodes on our cell phones. We guard the things we value for fear that someone else will swoop in and take possession of what rightfully belongs to us. What could be more precious than our own hearts?

Your heart is that core of your being, the center of the self where the *individual*—the one who cannot be divided—resides. Over time, ideas and images get imprinted on your mind and shape your thoughts, which shape your beliefs, which shape the essence of who you are. Your eyes and your ears are the gates that all outer signals travel through to reach your subconscious mind. From this day forward, guard them from the forces that seek to steal your peace and your power.

Mass media marketers understand the importance of getting through your gates. Consider the Super Bowl. Every year, Mars, Incorporated, spends millions of dollars for just a few seconds of screen time to make sure you catch a glance of their Snickers bar. Why do companies want your eyes so badly? The reason is they know that after the image enters into your thoughts, soon enough you'll be desiring their products. (I'm craving chocolate just thinking about it.)

Guard your gates.

Failure to do so will result in what the law of property calls "adverse possession." That's when a person loses title to their own land because they fell asleep on their property rights. When someone else uses the land openly and continuously for a certain length of time, it could legally become their land if the true owner does nothing.

Negativity works the same way. One minute you're in complete control, then it sneaks in quietly through the back door. You find yourself listening to a sad song about regretting the loss of a past lover. Before long, thoughts of your ex start to surface and your mood turns sour. While watching a television show about divorce, insecure thoughts about your partner's infidelity begin to surface. Or, after Netflix binging on scary movies with gruesome images, you find yourself becoming less empathetic. The safety of your gates requires eternal vigilance. What you see and hear can corrode your heart. If the people around you are unloving and unkind, in time their ways will graft onto your personality.

Challenge

Today use the phrase "off limits" as your alert slogan whenever you catch the wrong thoughts trespassing on your mind. Excuse yourself from the table if a conversation is not feeding your soul. Change the radio station if the song is not soothing your spirit.

Your heart is too valuable to permit just anyone or anything to have free access to it. Guard it by guarding your gates. You are a product of what you expose yourself to. If it does not elevate, demand it to evacuate your presence, post haste.

Soul Talk

I permit no negativity to intrude on my peace.
My heart is secure. My ears hear only good.
My eyes view only love. My gates are guarded.
I am safe.

8

The Question You Should Be Asking

"The unexamined life is not worth living..."
— Socrates

Before unlocking the laws of motion and gravitation, Sir Isaac Newton had to ask: "Why do objects fall?" Before creating a line of hair products for African Americans and becoming a millionaire, Madam C.J. Walker had to ask: "What's best for my hair?" Your level of joy and the quality of your life hinge on the caliber of questions you reflect on daily. No great discovery has ever happened without curiosity.

Questions direct your focus like a beam of light in a dark room. Most people spend their time asking the wrong questions. There may not be any stupid questions, but there are bicycle and pogo-stick questions. Pogo stick questions do just as the name implies, they *stick* and leave you stuck. They immobilize you because the answers they prompt bring you back down to where you started. "Why does this keep happening to me? When am I going to get over this person? What if I fail?" These are not empowering questions. They simply magnify the unwanted condition.

Bicycle questions have an objective. If you're pedaling on a bike, you're going in a specific direction. "How would I feel if I were the happiest person on Earth? How would I act if I were wealthy? If I were a confident person, what would I do in this situation?" These bicycle questions get your wheels of creativity turning and create momentum.

I once went to an app coding seminar hosted by my friend who partnered with Microsoft. He showed me how to build a game app using a simple coding language. The first thing I realized was the app would only do what I coded it do, nothing more. Likewise, our minds only do the tasks we steadily ask them to do. It's not enough to ask once. The first idea doesn't always light the light bulb. "I have not failed. I've found 10,000 ways that won't work," said Thomas Edison. You must ask yourself right questions over and over to produce right results.

Not all questions have to be about the future. The best questions bring you back to the all-important present moment. "Does what I'm doing right now make me fell good?" This question demands an immediate response and allows you to reassess your current condition. It is a reality check. When the answer is "no" for too long, you need to adjust or change your course completely.

Challenge

Ask yourself: "What do I want." Write it down. Ask yourself: "Why do I want it?" Write it down.

The question "what?" is your handlebar. It steers you in the right direction. The question "why?" is your pedal. It gives you the intention, and intention is what produces the energy necessary to get you where you want to go. One personal question I ask myself to get me back on track is: "What if what you're clinging to is hindering you from accessing all of the abundance God intends for your life?"

Soul Talk

I am done asking pogo-stick questions.
They do not serve me. I ask myself questions that move me toward more love, joy, peace, and prosperity.

9

The N-Word

Own your time, own your mind.
— love collins

It's OK to say it. It is the epitome of rejection. It is an electric fence that keeps out all intruders. Scarcely will you find someone who enjoys being told this, and many are hesitant to say it to others. The word is no.

Telling people "no" who you respect and care about can be uncomfortable. You may fear they will take it as a rejection of them personally. If you're the accommodating type, you probably say "yes" more than you ought to. You find yourself committing and overcommitting to the point where you can no longer divide your time into thinner slices. At some point, you're going to have to say "no" to them in order to say "yes" to you.

People will make withdrawal after withdrawal, if you let them. Their needs can quickly become your burdens and their emergencies can turn into your priorities. Don't go emotionally bankrupt trying to please everybody. Make a deposit into your own happiness. Maintaining your sanity requires knowing yourself and setting boundaries with an old fashioned "no".

Most people will tell you: "Don't overdo it. Don't exceed your limits." That advice, while well intended, won't lead you toward peace. Sure, frantic people always exceed their limits and exhaust themselves trying to feed every open mouth, but most people figure out what their limits are and walk right up to the line. They live in the *Almost Zone*. They are always almost ready to give up. They are almost at their wits end. They are almost drowning. Their nose is just above water. The way of peace is to live well within your exhaustion limit. Instead of telling yourself: "Yeah, I guess I could squeeze that into my schedule," just say "no". Introduce a new dialogue: "I want to have room to breathe and enjoy life. I don't want to tip toe right up next to my full line."

Challenge

If you have a calendar or daily planner with all your to-dos, start placing pockets of peace into your schedule. Carve out a time where you intentionally do nothing. When someone approaches you about taking on another task or joining another club, politely decline.

Your use of the N-word should not be a means of dodging responsibility. We all have duties to fulfill, chores to complete and people counting on us. A fellow writer once told me: "You have to be a warrior for your time." Own your time, own your mind. Great tasks require great focus. Your dream, your future, your goals all require time. For your gift to make room for you, you must make room for your gift.

Overcommitting won't allow you to do that. It won't make the people you've committed to any happier either when you inevitably let them down. They can tell you're not all in. They know when your mind is being pulled in all directions like a dog tied by his collar and his tail. They won't be satisfied with your half-heartedness. Why not give a few commitments 100 percent? In return, you'll master the habit of always giving your all.

Soul Talk

I am finally bold enough to say NO.
I will commit 100 percent to my commitments by accepting only what I can effectively take on.

10

Be Patient with You

"One minute of patience, ten years of peace."
— Greek Proverb

I've never seen grass grow. When I was about twelve years old, my friend Jimmy and I decided to mow lawns all summer so we could earn enough money to buy an Allen Iverson and a Tracy McGrady basketball jersey. My parents were our priority clients. After mowing a yard once, we couldn't wait for the grass to sprout up again so we could earn another five bucks apiece. Unfortunately, there was always a wait, and it was always too long.

You and I are just like the grass and, at the same time, just like little twelve-year-old landscapers who can't wait for it to grow. We look at where we are and see the gap between there and where we think we should be by now. We forget that growth is imperceptible in real time. No one sees grass growing. If you are not where you want to be yet, that means you are still on your way.

A roommate of mine at the University of Arkansas majored in architecture. Architects know that the taller the building, the deeper and wider the foundation must be. At its simplest form, construction consists of three stages: beginning, middle, and completion. I've heard countless people talk about how they wish they hadn't wasted so much time. "I would be so much further ahead in life," they say (and these are 20-something-year-olds). This quarter life crisis, much like the mid-life crisis, is universal. We want to skip over the beginnings and the middles and go straight to completions, but that's not architecturally feasible. Your building will fall if you try to skip steps. Now is the time for roots, not fruits. The final stage of your development will be marvelous but if you have not spent time learning what the valley is trying to teach you, how will you be prepared for the mountaintop?

Take a moment and consider how much more knowledgeable and mature you are now versus five years ago. Like the grass, you look up after a while and the change is unmistakable. You are expanding right now. The growth is slow by necessity. Just think of what would happen if you woke up tomorrow morning and you were ten feet tall. You would be stumbling all over the place and hitting your head on doorposts. Why? Because you weren't prepared for the sudden shift. This season you are in right now is called preparation. Learn more about yourself. What areas are you strong in? Which ones need exercise?

Challenge

Write a journal entry today detailing exactly how you feel. Write in it once a week. By the end of this year, you will look back and see how far you've come.

If you want to be a frog, don't get mad when God makes you a tadpole. Enjoy your metamorphosis. Allow yourself to fail. We don't get angry with a child who mispronounces words while learning to read. We don't yell and say: "Oh just shut up! You'll never get it." We say: "It's OK. Sound it out." Do that with you. Sound life out. You will be exactly where you always dreamed you'd be in due time.

Soul Talk

Today I will be patient with me. I will experience growth even if it's slow. I give myself permission to fail for I know the treasure of success is buried deep in the soils of failure.

11

The Two of Us

"A healthy body is a guest chamber for the soul:
a sick body is a prison."
— Francis Bacon

Mind and body. *And* not *or*. There's no separating the two. Can you remember a time when you were severely injured? Maybe it was just a minor injury that felt major in the moment, like hitting your shin on that metal bed railing. Your physical pain placed a direct strain on your emotional happiness. Physical pleasure has an equal and opposite effect. A big slice of red velvet cheesecake, for example, can turn my whole mood around. That's why it's called comfort food. That's why a massage leaves you feeling so relaxed. Your mental and bodily state are like a pair of conjoined twins. Make it your goal to create harmony between them.

Your body is a sacred place. The Bible describes it as a temple. "Do you not know that your bodies are temples of the Holy Spirit...?" (1 Corinthians 6:19). "To keep the body in good health is a duty," said the Buddha, "otherwise we shall not be able to keep our mind strong and clear." What are you putting into your mouth to keep your temple clean? You are what you eat, after all. Literally. The moment you place an orange wedge in your mouth, your body begins mechanical digestion as you crush the fruit with your teeth. You swallow. Your stomach breaks down the nutrients from the orange and distributes it throughout the rest of your body. At some point, the orange becomes a part of you.

Challenge

Take a long, loving look at everything you consume today. Ask yourself where it came from. The earth? A cow? Try to describe it. Is it green and alive or greasy and dead? How does your body respond when you eat it? Does it leave you feeling energetic or lethargic?

Remain conscious of what you eat this entire week. Notice the impact it has on your physiology and psychology. Does it make you feel true? By that I mean is it a reflection of what you want to be. Your body is primarily water, so water is our truest drink. Artificial foods and flavors are made to imitate nature, but they are not the real things. See if you can spot the truth and the lies on your dinner plate.

Slowly make a transition toward a more loving diet. Last year I told myself, I wanted to be a vegetarian because it's the best dietary plan for my blood type. I started off by getting rid of beef and then pork. I traded in my whole milk for almond and coconut milk. Now I've pushed aside all meat except seafood and eggs. The point is: baby steps are perfectly fine. You can climb a mountain one baby step at a time.

If working out for an hour a day seems impossible, start with a five-minute jog and a few stretches every morning to oil up your gears. Make exercise time social time by going with a friend or a family member a few days per week. When I go to the track field with my cousin Arnelle, we both work out harder than either of us would alone. Not only does the immediate rush of adrenaline after a run or weightlifting session enhance your mood, looking fit boosts your confidence and facilitates more mind-body harmony.

Soul Talk

Today I will treat my arms, my legs, and every inch of my body as sacred.
I will allow only the best to enter the best.

12

The Word Pool

"The tongue has the power of
life and death..."
— Proverbs 18:21

R id yourself of words that do not serve you. Words can seem harmless at first. If you hear someone speaking a foreign language, it's all just noise to you, but deep inside the ears of a native speaker are tiny little cells called "hair cells" that detect the vibrations and convert them into signals the brain reads as a sound. The same thing is happening inside of you, except their brain has given the sound meaning. What meanings have you given to your words?

"I'm working on getting up early," I said to a friend, referring to my New Year's Resolution.

"That was last year," she reminded me.

"Yeah, waking up is still tough for me," I replied.

Tough? At that moment, I realized why getting up early had been such a struggle. I had told myself the task was difficult, and it became so. That was my personal narrative, my story. But it was just that—a story. It was a fictional claim that had crystalized into truth. My words became my world.

"Words are things," said Maya Angelou, "They get in your rugs, in your upholstery, and in your clothes, and finally into you." There are nearly one million words in the English language. Most peoples' vocabularies consist of only about 20,000 words. Even though, it's estimated we speak about 16,000 words a day, most of us just recycle the same few. "Yes." "No." "Thanks." "You're welcome." "Hello." We all have a fleet of phrases we use almost automatically. When my friends tell me a great idea, my reply is usually: "That's dope." How's the party? "It's lit."

You probably have your own word pool. It's convenient to have words we can reach out and grab with ease. The problem is your pool can quickly get muddied with toxic words. How are things going? "They're going." "I had a bad day." "I'm not in a good mood right now." Those words sink into your subconscious and begin to manifest themselves even more definitively.

A young lady told me recently that she was not the type of person to get up in front of people. "I'm shy," she said. No, she isn't. She simply convinced herself that she's supposed to be shy. "Do you want me to say I'm not shy?"

Yes! That's exactly what I wanted her to say. Better yet, remove the negative: "I'm outgoing and bold." I wanted her to say it over and over. If you say anything long enough, even a lie, you will start to believe it. The more you start to believe something about yourself, the more others will affirm that belief.

Challenge

Make a list of words that you wish to eliminate from your vocabulary. For example, replace the word "problem" with challenge. There are no problems, only events or circumstance that challenge how innovative you are. Impossible, can't, never, boring, defeat, weak, and sad can all be buried.

Be very careful with the words you select and the truth you choose to accept. They could mean death or life. Words are like a fire. A fire can keep you warm, or a fire can burn you to ashes.

Soul Talk

My word pool will be purified today.
Because my words are so powerful, I will speak only words of life and peace.

13

Be Patient with People

*"Don't remove a fly from your friend's
forehead with a hatchet."*

— Chinese Proverb

Everyone is your mirror. Think of a person who you find extremely difficult to deal with—a parent, a child, a colleague, the barista at the café who always takes too long to make your coffee. Imagine them doing the very thing that annoys you most.

Now picture them as a little baby with wide, wet eyes, new to the monstrous world. Hear them crying and stretching their arms out for you to hold them. Let's be truthful. All of us are children deep down. You, me, everybody hides behind grown-up masks. A fragile innocence lives there. Be gentle with people. Know that the individual who annoys you most, no matter their age, has fears and hopes and goals and frailties just like you.

Even those who come off as coarse and im-penetrable have a soft spot of insecurity just beneath their icy surface. They're afraid too—afraid someone will poke at them and notice the truth of what's hidden. They wear the mask. For some, the need for acceptance and love is so intense that they telegraph confidence to hide the self-doubt. They talk loud and play the role of a big shot while they're inwardly screaming for significance.

Be patient with people because most are emotionally malnourished. As tempting as it may be to get angry and hostile, allow people to be exactly what they are—flawed. If you know more than them, teach don't taunt. Heal don't holler. Don't battle against their behavior. Resistance only takes away from your personal peace.

Every day you have a choice, nay, every moment. You may not be able to choose whom you work with or go to school or church with. You may not have any say whatsoever about the external events that occur or the attitudes that assail you, but you will always have the choice of response. You can return negativity for negativity or you can react with love and patience. Bask in the fact that no one can take that from you.

Challenge

When someone obnoxious or overbearing enters the room, silently say: "You may strike me, but I choose not to strike back. You can yell, but I choose to speak softly. You can do petty things to try to get under my skin, but your actions can never drain my positive energy."

If you try this and it still doesn't work, remember the *Art of Exit*. Get up and leave. Come back when you've cooled, and tell them honestly and lovingly exactly what they did to upset you. Then let go. Release. Practice surrendering your need to have everyone around you conform perfectly to your predetermined expectations and desires. Love them as they come.

Soul Talk

Today I am patient with the people around me.
I know they are just innocent children draped
in the costumes of adult men and women.
I will love them and respond with compassion.

14

The Graveyard

The fear of death follows from the fear of life.
A man who lives fully is prepared to die at any time.
— Mark Twain

This morning I walked past them. This evening, as I peeped through my blinds, those same white marble tombstones from the Fayetteville National Cemetery were still stuck across the street. The same chorus of silence echoed. Hundreds of voices that once chanted at football games and sang in the car when no one was around are now trapped beneath the ground my eyes leisurely look over.

How is death supposed to make you more positive? It may not. What it will do is make you more mindful. It will return you home to the fact that your life is like a milk carton—stamped with an expiration date. How many people were in a rush for work on their final morning? Which of them forgot to tell their spouse how much they loved them? Who died with unfulfilled dreams? The graveyard is full of once busy people. They drank coffee to stay awake. They skipped meals. They were in a rush, just like us. Because they never remembered death, many forgot to live.

Think of all the little things that consume the minutes and hours of your day. How much time do you spend mentally reviewing all the tasks you need to complete? Which of the items on your to-do list would matter if you died today? Probably very few. A trip, real or mental, past the grave-yard can quickly re-shuffle the most important aspects of your life back to the top. When you confront the reality and inevitability of death, your perspective widens. You see the entire gar-den and not just the annoying weeds. Sure, your day was hectic, but your family still loves you.

There's a friend who is thinking about you but is too afraid to bother you because you're always busy. Stop and breathe. Your body is begging you for a break anyways. Your eyes wish you would take them to see a play or a sunset. Your nose longs to sniff a flower or sip the salty smell of the sea. Your hands want to be held.

The trivial things that consume your life dis-tract your mind from the thought of eternity. In a hundred years, most of the stuff you thought about today won't matter. No one will remember your grade point average. The world will have forgotten how much money you made. (Your great grandkids will probably have spent every penny.) This may seem depressing. The thought of all the hours worked and labored one day being meaningless is tragic, but it's also liberating. You can be free to focus on more lasting matters, like how much love you deposited into the universe with your life. What values and memories did you preserve and pass on to others that will empower future generations?

Your life has meaning, and you are here for a purpose. When you feel inner dissatisfaction, it's usually because you're not at your *12 o'clock*. That's where a new day begins. It's where the hour and minute hand embrace each other. It's your center. Disharmony comes when two pieces of you conflict. One part, like a minute hand, hurries in a direction away from your essence. Spin the dial. Reset your internal perspective to the 12 o'clock position where you are most on purpose and fulfilled (fully filled). This is where you're living truly instead of artificially contorting your life into what others want it to be and doing meaningless task that don't serve your destiny.

Soul Talk

I will live purposefully because I am mindful that my time is precious. I have come here with my pitcher of potential filled to the brim. I will pour every drop and die empty.

15

The Flexible Fox

"In such cases, slight modifications, which in any way favoured the individuals of any species, by better adapting them to their altered conditions, would tend to be preserved."

— Charles Darwin

Childhood crawls into adulthood. Winter mornings bloom into spring afternoons. Waves ebb and flow. Clouds come and go. You too are coming and going. You're not who you were last year. In fact, you're probably not the same person you were yesterday. The perpetuation of life demands evolution and change.

Still, change can be terrifying. By definition it implies discomfort and a shaking of the status quo. Our place of comfort is where we are the most peaceful. The tension of change creates in us a feeling of vertigo and dissonance. We resist. The more you resist, however, the more tormenting change feels. Were you ever so scared to get a shot as child that you looked away when the doctor or nurse injected the needle? In the end, you didn't even realize she had stuck you. Other times, when you watched her slowly pierce the needle into your skin, it seemed unbearable. Your arms got tense. Your fist balled. Your eyebrows lowered. Your nose crinkled.

Resistance and inflexibility are pain enhancers not pain killers. One way to cultivate a mind that is open and bendable is through stretching techniques like yoga. Gaining more physical flexibility can loosen the stiff muscles in your mind. Stretching extends the tense spots in your body that are so used to sitting at a computer, driving in a car, and sleeping flat on a bed. When you feel loose and light, you can hover over change. You can "levitate," as rapper Kendrick Lamar put it. The cares and troubles of the world appear, but you do not despise them or beg them to leave. You simply greet them with a friendly wave and wait for them to disappear again.

Challenge

Switch up your day. Take a less familiar route to work or back home. Randomly leave town and go visit a friend or family member. Try that new restaurant you've passed by for weeks. Do something to experience new sensory inputs.

Adaption to change is not just the path to peace; it is vital for survival. For instance, the

Arctic fox lives in the cold tundra of Alaska. It's fur changes colors as the seasons change. During spring and summer, it wears a dark coat to match the ground. When the snow comes, a white coat of fur grows over the grey so it can blend in with the snowy tundra. The camouflage helps it elude predators and ultimately keeps it alive.

Temperatures in your life will fluctuate. Your environment will change, but when the winter comes, you can do as the Arctic fox and put on a new coat. Cast aside all the rigid, inflexible thoughts of control. Catch, then release. The need to control your environment is limiting. You will begin to have more expansive thoughts and bountiful experiences as you allow life to surprise you with its little gifts of wonder.

Soul Talk

The world is changing.
I am connected to the world, so I am changing.
I will not fight against the whole world and myself. Today I will adapt and thrive.

16

Be Magnetic

"We become what we think about all day long."
— Ralph Waldo Emerson

Think about it. Have you ever noticed how certain people always seem to be happy and positive? Success and prosperity strangely gravitates in their direction. Then there are others who you already know, the moment they approach you, have a long, dramatic story to tell about their latest troubles. Why is that? How come some people can't seem to win and others can't seem to lose?

In one word: thoughts.

Like magnets, each thought produces a force field inside our minds. This field is either negatively or positively charged. Everyone knows that a magnet can attract certain metals and repel others. When you think a negative thought and allow it to linger in your mind, other negative thoughts are pulled towards it.

Think of a time you felt sad. Chances are you started to feel frustrated soon after, then angry, then guilty, and eventually depressed because you were experiencing so many negative emotions. Bad thoughts compound. Equally, thoughts of happiness and love breed more goodness. Better thoughts attract better people and better opportunities. Who doesn't love being around someone who is motivated and inspired? Their energy energizes you. It's infectious.

So does this mean you're not allowed to think even one bad thought? No. It simply means you must not permit your mind to dwell on negativity. It is your mind after all. Consider how much control you posses. Ball your fist. Blink your eyes. Tap your foot. See how instantaneously you can command your body to act in accordance with what you desire?

The same is possible for your mind. Most of the time we're on autopilot. We don't have to think when we drive to work. Our minds already know the route and the speed limit. We don't have to think about how to bathe ourselves or eat. We just do it. Often, because of old patterns, negative thoughts just come over uninvited. You can't stop them from coming. You can only become aware of them and gently usher them toward the door when they arrive.

Ask yourself how you feel right now. That is the biggest indicator of your present thought life. If you feel amazing, you're probably already thinking amazing thoughts. If you are stressed, worried, or fearful, see if you can transition your focus from what scares you to what your first move would be if you weren't scared.

Challenge

Think positively for one hour straight today.

When I first started practicing this technique, I became hypersensitive to my thoughts. I couldn't go five minutes. I got stressed out even more when I realized how negative they really were. Eventually, I had to accept that this was part of the process. At least I was not blind anymore to what was going on in my own head. I was patient with myself, and one day I realized almost all of my thoughts were positive and peaceful. Your magnets can attract everything you want—more joy, more confidence, and more people around you who desire the same things. Be magnetic.

Soul Talk

Today I am committed to thinking lovely thoughts. I will repel all negativity and attract only the best.

17

The Man in the Dark Jacket

"Poor, yet making many rich; having nothing,
and yet possessing everything."
— 2 Corinthians 6:10

A man in a dark jacket was buying a book. A woman with long, blonde hair was ordering coffee. A girl was studying. Two men near the exit were discussing business, and I was reading silently in the café section of the bookstore. All of a sudden, an older gentleman, about my father's age by the looks of him, walked up to me and said: "Hello, young man."

"Hello, stranger who I've never met," I thought to myself. He commented on the Maya Angelou book lying beside me and then asked what I drink when I'm at the café. Green tea, usually. He walked to the counter and yelled back at me, "Iced or hot?" "Uhh, iced," I said, still puzzled. I looked away for a minute, and the barista delivered a large cup of iced green tea to my table. When I turned around to thank the man, he was gone.

I was the victim of a random act of kindness. He wasn't looking for thanks or recognition, he simply wanted to be nice, just because. When you are kind for no reason at all towards people, it completely throws them off balance. They won't know how to respond to such kindness without condition. Most of us, Americans at least, are hard-wired capitalists who expect to give something in return when a benefit is conferred. Most of our day-to-day transactions are acts of obligation not altruism.

Whether that is bad or good, who knows? I do know that giving is a breach of the status quo that leaves the receiver feeling significant. It means so much to feel valued. Just as one negative incident can ruin your day, one small gesture of affection can leave you feeling euphoric for hours. An even deeper joy, however, lies in knowing you created that feeling inside of someone else. When you infect a person with kindness by dropping them off at home or helping them with homework or opening a door, your own prescription of joy is refilled. Those who give the most tend to get the most.

Mother Teresa of Calcutta, a woman who devoted her life to helping people who are financially poor, said to Nodlaig McCarthy: "I have never been in need. But I accept, I never refuse what people give...I accept whatever. So having nothing, yet possessing all things." The generous heart always seems to have more to give. Operate from a place of abundance. Imagine you are already rich. Now behave that way. Imagine you have more love than any one person could ever consume. Now share it.

Challenge

Commit a random act of kindness today. Then try to forget you did it. Keep it a secret from everyone, even yourself. Give and forget.

The desire to broadcast your generosity is just the ego kicking in. Your brain wants the quick hit of dopamine that comes from a pat on the back and quiet affirmation from those around you. It ends up fouling your good intentions. The goal is not to gain approval but to nurture your soul through the practice of shining a light in someone's darkness. See giving as a privilege not an obligation.

Soul Talk

My heart is filled with the fullness of compassion. I do acts of kindness because I am kind. The happiness of others makes me happy.

18

The Real You

"Live with a steady superiority over life..."
— Aleksandr Solzhenitsyn

Step back. Pry yourself from your own emotions, and you will realize that you are not upset. You are not stressed. You are not worried. You are not depressed. You are not a feeling. You are a human *being* who experiences moods the way the sky experiences rainbows. A rainbow is the result of sunlight dispersed throughout droplets of water in the air. Rainbows are not permanent. Like emotions, they appear and disappear. Whether they come or go, the sky remains.

In the heat of anger, it seems as if *you* are angry, but you are not the anger. Emotions are temporary and external, but your essence is internal and eternal. Consider how you feel this very second. What color is the rainbow in your clouds? A blue sadness? A red passion? A yellow calm? The moment you can consciously identify and examine your current state is the moment you can regain control of it.

You have the power to say to yourself: "This is not me." Your mood is not a cause; it is an effect.

If you want a new effect, you must replace the old cause. Honestly, some causes are beyond your control. Some bad news may hit you unexpectedly and send you into a rage or a fit of tears. That's OK. Your body is the best way to identify what state you are in emotionally. The tears are your body's way of telling your mind: "We are sad right now."

The next step is crucial. It determines whether you will rule or be ruled. You can allow the feeling to soak, or you can counter it with an equal and opposite reaction. If your mouth is frowning, respond with a smile. Greet your tears with laughter. Meet your fears with massive action. If you are uncertain, instead of slouching over and looking the part, stand up straight and tall and speak loudly. These are just a few bodily antidotes for the most common and undesirable of emotions.

Treatment is still not nearly as good as prevention. Good emotions can be created. Try this technique.

Challenge

This evening, tomorrow morning, or one day this week that you expect to be extra challenging, get really dressed up. I'm talking

Sunday's best. Blazer, tie clip, socks. Heels, earrings, dress. Convince yourself that if you look good you will feel good.

Watch your walk get a little more confident. Your back and shoulders will straighten. People will smile at you more. Instead of letting your mood control your actions, dressing up will be the action that helps you control your mood.

Soul Talk

I am eternal. My moods are fleeting.
They are not me; they are mine.
I choose which emotions to banish and which to keep. Love. Joy. Peace. I keep these.

19

Laugh

You may be going through your own civil war
on the inside. Fight it with laughter.
— love collins

It was the fall of 1862. America was bloody. Hundreds of thousands had been killed or wounded in battle. The freedom of slaves and the future of the republic hung in the balance. Meanwhile, President Abraham Lincoln was laughing. Members of his war cabinet in the room were not amused. "Gentlemen," he said, "Why don't you laugh? With the fearful strain that is upon me night and day, if I did not laugh, I should die, and you need this medicine as much as I do."[i]

Laughter is not just medicine; it is oxygen. Humans are among the few creatures with the gift of laughter. It is a rare language that nature has graciously taught us to speak. There can be no doubt that the Civil War was one of the saddest, most frightful moments in United States history. It would seem to be a terrible time to engage in humor, but the truth is: laughter is necessary to ward off despair. When we laugh a stomach-twisting laugh, our bodies release hormones known as endorphins, which alleviate pain.

How many times have you laughed today? Typically, our negative feelings are just stomach growls from the soul warning us that we need to feed ourselves a helping of laughter.

Laugh at life. Laugh at yourself. One morning I was running to catch the bus and had almost made it when I realized I forgot my cell phone and my book at the room. I had to turn back. Since the bus was long gone by that point, I decided I might as well grab some blueberry yogurt for breakfast. A few bites in, I stood up and my cup of yogurt splattered all across the carpet. I was furious for a moment.

Then I laughed.

The laughter made me forget my anger. Although tragedy and comedy are opposites, they live on the same spectrum. Every negative incident can be viewed through the lens of comedy, even when you are dealing with an unspeakable circumstance. You need comedy all the more in tragedy. Today you may be going through your own civil war on the inside.

Fight it with laughter.

Challenge

Wake up to laughter. Look up a clip of your favorite comedian on YouTube. Find a funny meme. Follow comedians who posts videos regularly on Facebook like my favorites, Wayne Colley and Steve Harvey.

The morning joy will spread into your afternoon. At lunch, take another laugh break. Notice how much more pleasurable your meal is when you sit with friends and share laughs. Go to bed to laughter.

Soul Talk

I will live a life of laughter.
At the good, the bad, the mean, and the in between, I will laugh.
I will find the humor in every situation.

20

The Neat Freak

The places you eat, sleep, bathe and nourish your body ought to be worthy of the temple they support. Simply.

— love collins

This morning I left my dreams and began cleaning. The entire week felt like a load. Scattered thoughts were strewn across my mind like the dirty clothes on the floor or the dishes in my sink. I did not realize how deeply the physical clutter around me had seeped into my subconscious. It was not until hours later, with my apartment spotless for the first time in more days than I wish to admit, that I finally felt free.

Free yourself from clutter. If your body is your temple, then your living space is the holy ground it sits upon. Your eyes are tiny camera lenses that allow you to view the world, but if the image they see is not one of beauty, how can they tell your mind to think beautiful thoughts?

When you examine your room, your car, or your workspace, what do you see? Are there any loose papers you could trash or items not serving a purpose? Get rid of them. At any given time, you can find television commercials or billboards begging you to buy items you have absolutely no need for. The world is engrossed with accumulating more. It says, "The more you own, the happier, more successful you will be."

The opposite is true. The less "stuff" outside of yourself that you need, the more peaceful and whole you will feel. The goal is *simplicity*. Ask yourself: "What can I do without?" As you begin to clean up your living space, you'll find things you haven't used in weeks or months. A part of you will want to hold on to some of it because it's yours.

Maybe you have dropped your phone before and it shattered. You probably felt a flash of pain inside. On a certain level, the phone had become a part of you. When you get rid of excessive attachments, you are reminded that the things you have are yours, not you. They exist outside of you. You can throw away an old notebook and not evaporate. You can give away some dated clothes, and your bones will remain in tact. You don't have to be possessed by possessions.

Simplify. It's easy to get busy and neglect something as minute as cleaning up. It's so small, so seemingly insignificant. "I'll get to it later," you say. Meanwhile, the mess just gets messier. You eventually reach the point where just walking into your kitchen or bathroom triggers negative emotions.

Challenge

When you enter your sanctuary, enter beauty. Place a picture or painting on the wall that inspires you. Spray a pleasant scent so that when you walk through the door, a smile sweeps under your nose. Turn on some soft music. Get candles or a lava lamp to create an environment of tranquility in your most intimate space.

You may know people who tell their visitors to remove their shoes at the door. It's not petty. It's a way to honor your home. The places you eat, sleep, bathe, and nourish your body ought to be worthy of the temple they support. Simplify. Free yourself of the little excesses that lead to mental litter and restless thoughts.

Soul Talk

I will treat my living space as sacred ground.
I will keep it empty of clutter so my mind can stay full of peace.

21

The Taste Bud

You have to learn to see into the future. Yes, it may feel
good now, but what are the side effects?
— love collins

Why don't carrots taste like chocolate? Why doesn't banana pudding taste like Brussels sprouts? Life would be so much easier if the things that are good for us were the most enticing and the things that are bad for us were repulsive. Diets wouldn't exist. Staying healthy would be effortless. Spouses wouldn't cheat. Drug dealers would go out of business. If only our physical and emotional taste buds craved only what was best for us.

A group of friends and I went for ice-cream in D.C., and one of the girls with us was lactose intolerant. She started to order, and we all turned in shock. "It's fine. I brought Pepto-Bismol," she said, giggling. She loved the taste of dairy so much that even though she knew it would cause her extreme discomfort later that night, she was willing to exchange a moment of present pleasure for hours of future suffering. How often do you do this?

Drama. Negativity. Distractions. As damaging as they are, we seem naturally attracted to them. Reality television and tabloid talk shows that highlight rebellious teens or expose abusive spouses and shameful sex secrets dominate day-time television. Most people could sit for hours watching couples argue but fall asleep during a lecture on how to end hunger. Why is it? Taste buds.

Picture your favorite dessert on a plate in front of you right now. Try to recall when you first decided that it was your favorite. It's proba-bly been so long you can barely remember, but your taste buds never forgot. Now think of your least favorite food. For me, it used to be okra, but the older I got the more I began to like it. My taste buds changed.

To attract more love, peace, and positivity, you must desire the things that produce them. Some people chew on the hard candy of negativ-ity so long that it leaves cavities. Others have the taste of drama tattooed on their tongue. Thank-fully, anyone can rewire their desire.

You have to learn to see into the future. Yes, it may feel good now, but what are the side effects? Will giving in to that habit be worth the destruc-tion it causes to your family? How tasty will that food be when you step on the scales next week?

Often the misery of the situation hides like a groundhog and then pops up when all the pleasure has passed. Don't be deceived. It only makes sense that something toxic would tempt you. The right thing rarely ever comes packaged in a box with a big red bow and a note attached saying: "Open me." Meaningless conversations and fruitless complaints are the ones who strut through the door demanding attention. Recognize negativity and flee from it.

Ultimately, your desire isn't just about you. If you don't assert control of over your taste buds, they will control your future and thwart the great work that only your hands can create. You may have to clean out some cabinets. You may have to exile the people who are poisonous and the places that trigger the wrong desires within you.

Soul Talk

People will say I'm changing. I am.
I'm taking on a new form.
Like milk to ice cream, I'm different. I think differently. I no longer desire to do the things I used to do or go the places I used to go.
I have new standards, new taste buds.

22

Be Quiet

"Isolation is the gift."
— Charles Bukowski

You are like the letter *I*. It is the only letter of the alphabet that always gets capitalized when it is alone. Sometimes solitude is a necessary for growth. Sometimes your season of singleness is a gift. Don't swim from your island too quickly.

Most people view separation as punishment. A child who misbehaves is sent to a corner for timeout. An inmate on death row gets placed in solitary confinement. Yes, we are social beings who need interaction. And yes, too much time spent alone can cause psychological decay, but a little quiet time is essential for personal elevation. If peace were a sound it would be silence.

Have you ever been to a concert or a party where the music was so loud that when you got home hours later your ears rang? The noise was so annoying that you had to create more noise just to drown it out. Your eardrums desperately long for silence just as your mind yearns for peace.

Silence allows you to renew your mind. It's like a nap for your ears, which never get a break. Your eyes shut. Your mouth closes. Even your palm can squeeze into a quiet fist, but your ears are always open, always receiving. That's why an alarm clock can wake you up (well, unless you sleep as hard as a frozen rock, like me). When you are alone in a room with nothing but your own breath, the life entering and exiting your body commands complete attention. You are sucked back into the present moment.

Challenge

Pick a day this week when you have no obligations or plans, and be silent. Call your parents, your children, or your best friend and tell them you're going to be quiet for a day. If they call and you don't answer, they'll know why.

A whole day of silence? Absolutely. I did this for 24 hours once. I quickly realized how stressful it could be when you're stuck inside your own head. Truthfully, I broke the silence about three times. I would start singing a tune in my head and before I knew it I was belting the lyrics. I even caught myself yelling at my computer screen.

If you can't set aside an entire twenty-four hours, carve out twenty-four minutes today to greet peace in your quiet place. You'll see that it feels like taking a walk with an old friend you haven't seen in years or sipping a drink you seldom taste. In your time of silence, notice how the world goes on without you. It doesn't skip a beat. You, too, are free to go on without the world as you take sips of silence.

Soul Talk

Today I will stop running from myself.
The place of growth is lonely and quiet, but it is a gift. It is a friend. I am grateful for my gifts and my friends.

23

The Sound Came First

Courage is what it takes to stand up and speak; courage is also what it takes to sit down and listen."

— Winston Churchill

You knew nothing. You were yanked from your mother's belly and dropped into a new world after months of darkness. You heard laughs and chatter with your ears, but your brand new brain could not yet decipher the sounds. You kept listening.

Peace begins with open ears. How many times have you found yourself talking over someone or completing their sentences? We all do it, and none of us can stand when others do it to us. The practice of listening allows you to shed your ego, which is the cause of most sufferings. It is the part of you that believes you must be heard and acknowledged. When it is not given total attention, it causes you to feel discontent and neglected. Ironically, when your ego is starved, the hunger for attention eventually disappears. The emptiness becomes so filling—more space in your mind for wisdom.

Instead of being frantic to get your point across or convince others to agree with your point of view, find peace and power in restraint. Listening is not just a passive procedure of receiving but an affirmative act of giving. We all know the euphoria that comes from helping someone in need. The whole world is in need of being heard. The greatest kindness you can offer anyone is to listen.

I heard two men passionately arguing over the radio about police and community relationships. They were both so determined to speak that neither was truly tuned into the other. A civilized conversation became a shouting match. Interruption after interruption proceeded and chaos came, not peace.

"Let every person be quick to hear, slow to speak," says Scripture. Who can learn while talking? Listening helps mature your spirit of humility. Students listen to their teacher because the teacher has information that the student is not yet privy to.

Challenge

Pretend today that everyone you meet is a master sensei who holds deep truths. You are the student. Listen to them—to their words and their body language. Note the sounds and ideas you pick up. Seek wisdom. Seek understanding.

Soul Talk

Today I will listen.
I will hear in a new way as I give others the honor of speaking.
Their words are precious and they have so much to teach me.

24

The 1-Hour Rule

"The early morning has gold in its mouth."
— Benjamin Franklin

Y ou don't need a time machine. You don't need
a secret pill or a magic fountain to lengthen
your life. You already have the ability to add more
living to your days by simply waking up a little
earlier. More time means less rushing. Less
rushing means more peace. More peace means a
more positive attitude. This is such an obvious
and familiar formula yet virtually everyone ig-
nores it.

Most people arise to the roaring of the third or
fourth alarm on their cell phones. They get up in a
frenzy, rushing through breakfast and sprinting to
their destination. This might describe you too. It
definitely portrays what my mornings looked like
prior to one life-altering decision: *I will arise at
5:30 every morning.*

My usual time during law school was around
6:30 a.m. or 6:45 a.m., just enough time for me to
catch the 7:15 a.m. shuttle and make it to my 8:00
a.m. class. There was no time to think, no time to
reflect and, most days, no time to eat. There was
something I didn't fully understand:

Rising early is easy.

Correction: rising early is easy when you *want* to rise early. The issue is most people have zero desire to do it because sleep is pleasurable. Getting up is usually mandatory. You wake up and start justifying why you deserve a few more minutes of rest. All that debating and reasoning with your emotions during those few seconds while the alarm rings is what keeps you tied to the mattress.

After those first few moments, your comfort mechanisms kick in and you are powerless. Start seeing those initial seconds for what they truly are: hours, potentially days, of lost life. If you remain asleep and miss those precious minutes of reflection before your day starts, you may never think of that business idea which could make you millions of dollars. You may rush out the house without wishing your family member a happy birthday, leaving them feeling forgotten.

Challenge

Apply the 1-Hour Rule. Wake up one hour earlier than you normally do. Instead of lingering in bed, get up and get in motion.

Stretch and do a few sit-ups (or push-ups, if you're feeling frolicsome). Spend time doing your morning gratitude and self-affirmations. Finally, spend five minutes in silence, simply ushering in the new day.

Yes, the morning has gold on its tongue. The sheer view of the night sky changing from black to blue to orange is revitalizing. It is your opportunity to see how swiftly time moves and your chance to cultivate the garden of your soul.

Soul Talk

I am an early riser. I rise with the same energy as the sun. I have the same powers.
My day will be just as brilliant.
My light will be so bright that others will see its radiance and grow, like flowers.

25

Be about that Action

"In order to act you must be somewhat insane.
A reasonably sensible man is satisfied with thinking."
— Georges Clémenceau

To all things there is a *kairos.* To all things there is an opportune time—a moment to be still and a moment move, a moment to prepare and a moment to perform. Most of our inner battles are brought about when we willfully let ourselves down and miss our moments. We say we're going to get it done, but we don't. We talk about what we should accomplish yet we procrastinate.

Each time you break your promise, your self-belief diminishes. Slowly, it melts like a glacier in the sun. Before you know it you are sinking into a place of lukewarm neutrality. The excuses get more and more believable. Finally, you are stuck. Anything that sits in one place too long molds and decays.

I love my grandmother. As a child, I would sit at her house for hours and watch *The Price is Right* game show during the summer. After that went off, her favorite soap opera would come on—*The Young and the Restless.* She would always watch from her reclining armchair. Sometimes she would let me sit there when she was outside or washing dishes. The longer I sat the lazier I became. Eventually she would reappear. "Alright, get out of my seat." I knew I had about two seconds to comply—or else. You don't have much more time than that before your excuses start to smother you. Do something today that the future you will be thankful for: Attack!

The antidote for procrastination is massive action. The more you do the more you want to do. Newton's First Law is always at play: "An object at rest stays at rest and an object in motion stays in motion with the same speed and in the same direction unless acted upon by an unbalanced force." Most people are paralyzed by inertia and fail to make the first step. The first step is just a sheep in a lion's costume. It appears scary and intimidating, but once you make it, you realize you could have made ten thousand more by now had you simply arrested your fears. Fear is the enemy of peace and growth.

You need growth. You need motion. Motion creates momentum. I've heard millionaires explain that the reason why they keep working well into their old age is because doing nothing is miserable. That's why slumps are so depressing. There is no growth in a slump.

"All it takes is one *now* to end a cycle of *nevers*," my friend Alec once told me. Your happiness and your potential peace are trapped behind your willingness to act now.

Challenge

When you are in need of momentum, let the spark to your action be this thought: "If I do not act now, I may never know how far I was meant to fly."

That's frightening—to get to the end of your life and look back wishing you had done what you were too afraid or too lazy to do.

Soul Talk

I have been still long enough.
Today I will act! I will not act tomorrow for tomorrow is fiction. It is a story unwritten.
I will act right here, right now, in this kairos.

26

The Tiny Emptiness

*"Life is a daring adventure
or nothing at all."*
— Hellen Keller

Children are so full of dreams. "I'm going to be a truck driver, a farmer, and a preacher," my cousin Keilan told me when he was twelve. Kids can imagine the most wonderful versions of how they would like their lives to go. As we grow older, many of us part ways with the believers we once were.

The world gets bigger and our goals get smaller, more *realistic.* At some point you wake up and notice you have almost stopped dreaming. Almost. The dreamer within you is not yet completely comatose. A spark of belief is still there. A rush of joy comes over you every time you cook a meal. "I always did want to be chef," you remember. A warmth rises from your belly to you cheeks whenever you walk into a library. "What if I really did write that book?"

Most people never live their dreams and not because the skill isn't there but because the faith isn't. They don't think they deserve to do what they love. Society is somewhat to blame. We are trained to live within limits. Your car can proba-bly go over 160 miles per hour, but there's nowhere in America you could ever drive that fast—legally. Speed limits are in place to slow you down. Self-doubt does the same thing.

You possess within you the potential to live a no-limit life right now. There is something you absolutely love to do. Everyone already knows it. You're great at it, and if you really committed to it, you could be phenomenal. Yet you don't.

You justify your inaction with reasons why you're to busy or too tired. The truth is you're too afraid. You can feel that tiny emptiness inside when you haven't done it in a while. This self-torment can strip you of your peace. Sadly, no technique or positive affirmation can fix this root issue. The only solution is for you to carve out time daily to practice your passion.

Do you need to draw for fifteen minutes? Must you work in the garden for an hour after work? Should you sit down at the piano before you go to bed or write poems at daybreak every morning? Well, wake up. Get it done.

This is not just advice for you. This is a warn-ing I had to give to myself. I know that empty feeling all too well. I have floated like a cloud in search of brighter skies, instead of making room for the sunshine. Years before this book was ever birthed, I told my friends and family about the idea. Weeks passed. Then months. Occasionally, someone would say: "So what about that book?" "It's coming," I'd reply, knowing good and well not a single page was written. Eventually, not doing what I loved started tearing me apart inside. When I finally committed, I spent hours at the public library after class and on weekends for months. It felt like minutes. I felt the weight lifting

You are gifted in order to give. How many songs have you almost sang? How many lives have you almost lived? Don't wait. Your joy and serenity will fill up the moment you give yourself permission to do what you love.

Soul Talk

> *Today I will do what I love.*
> *I give myself permission to*
> *live fully and dream.*

27

The Map

*"I had crossed the line. I was free; but there was no one
to welcome me to the land of freedom.
I was a stranger in a strange land."*

— Harriet Tubman

Today the world will tug you. It will try to pull and pry your time and attention from your grasp. If you are not vigilant, you might mis-locate yourself. You can get lost in the deadlines and to-do lists. Your lust for productivity can send you feasting on things that leave you starving. You find yourself in a maze with no exit.

Self-location is when you develop a conscious awareness of the space you occupy on this planet. It is where you are at this moment. Your physical, emotional, and spiritual coordinates are mapped entirely by you. Sometimes, though, it may not feel that way. The number of assignments to complete, meetings to attend, and emails to answer is endless. "Where am I?" This is the question to ask yourself when your grip begins to slip.

One spring I was traveling to the lake. As I approached, I could see the trail winding around the water so I decided to walk the path that led up to the boating dock. When I parked my car in the gravel parking area, the lake was nowhere in sight. Trees littered the landscape. I was lost. I walked toward the trail entrance and noticed a map that had "you are here" stamped on the center. Suddenly I knew exactly where to go.

Where are you? Be honest. Are you lost in someone else's expectations of who you should be? Is your focus so fixed on the lives of others that you have lost sight of your own? Many people lose themselves in the image of who they think they ought to be or who they want the world to perceive them as. Really, most people could care less about you. They are just as self-absorbed and fearful of judgment.

You are here. You do not need to try to be special. You already are special. You don't need to measure up to anyone. It's better to be yourself and barefoot than to walk with shoes on in someone else's footsteps. Their sneakers are probably too small for your feet anyway. Retire from trying to meet all the demands of others. In the end, even if you do manage to please everyone and check everything off your list today, tomorrow you'll have a new list and new people who want to be satisfied.

Harriet Tubman had to travel dozens of miles under the midnight sky and dodge slave catchers to find her way to the freedom. It was only then that she was able to free others. Locate yourself first. Do the inner work so that you can proceed to the outer.

The key is learning how to focus. So often we try to do ten things at once. "The man who chases two rats catches neither," said Confucius. Allow yourself to settle into this moment and this task at hand.

Challenge

Light a candle or sit a glass of water in front of you. Focus your entire attention on the flame or the liquid. Remain still and contemplative for five minutes. Do this daily. Teach your mind to focus.

Soul Talk

I am here.
I am capable only of being in one physical location at once. If I try to be everywhere and do everything, I may lose myself.
I am here. Here is peace.

28

Be Powerful

"The older I get, the greater power I seem to have
to help the world; I am like a snowball –
the further I am rolled the more I gain.
— Susan B. Anthony

Later that night, at dinner, she lost her power. A colleague of mine grew angry after her former co-worker walked through the door. She had worked closely with this individual and personally witnessed him demean and degrade clients, most of whom earned incomes below the poverty threshold. "They are so stupid," he told her. That comment shook her to the core. "It made me sick."

How often has someone else's actions, comments, or very presence altered your entire mood? One person's face can send you into a fury while another person's smile can light up your day. If they can *make* you happy, they can make you miserable. No one deserves that much power over you. You are already *made.* A healthy, wholesome relationship is not based on force; it should *bring* not *make.* See their actions as offerings. If they *bring* you joy, receive it. If they *bring* stress or drama, simply reject them.

"No, thank you," says my soul.

As you shift your perspective from being made to feel to being offered to receive a particular feeling, you make a step toward independence and freedom. It is easy to mistake dependency for devotion. To hinge your soul on the unpredictable impulses of another is slavery. In ancient times, no one dared bother the king when he was angry for fear of being put to death. To place your happiness in someone's care other than your own is to risk the assassination of your peace.

Take back your power. Who or what is it in your life right now that has too much control? If you have paused in a place of passivity, afraid of their force, now is the time to confront the truth. If your situation is like my colleague with the belligerent co-worker, you may need to address the person and inform them that their words are offensive and hurtful. This may not stop them, but it will embolden you. It will shift you from powerless to powerful.

If someone has hurt you so deeply that you can't bear the sight of that person, it may be time to sit down and have a healing conversation. They may not even know they have caused you grief. So often people are unconscious of the micro-wounds they inflict. Break down the wall of pain with an open door of dialogue and forgiveness.

Jesus instructed his followers to "love your enemies." Loving your enemies is like saying: "Even though you have brought me hate, I bring you compassion. You no longer control me."

Soul Talk

I control me.
My power is mine. My joy is mine.
I am made free.
No one can undo or remake me.
Only when they "bring" me peace and love will I accept their offerings.

29

The Shoes Ain't the Sidewalk

"There is only time for loving and but an instant so to speak for that."

— Mark Twain

We are walking through a city of seven billion. Sadly, there is more concern for shoes than sidewalks. Shoes are valuable. When worn, they can protect your feet from the sizzling hot concrete. They can offer comfort and aesthetic appeal, but they are not the path. The sidewalk is what will lead you to your destination. Without the sidewalk, shoes are nothingness.

More money, more fame, and more achievements can fill, but they are not fulfilling. We all know this but still we crave and cling to them. We make them our primary objectives, but that's all they are—objects. They are shoes. The peace and contentment you seek is reachable only by the sidewalk of meaningful connections—with family, with friends, with strangers, with God. This requires intimacy, and intimacy is the hard, ugly interior of love.

Yes, it would be easier if a short puff of attention or money could bring lasting satisfaction, but it can't. You need deep relationships not peripheral ones. Don't isolate yourself on an island so far from people that you forget the joy of human interaction. Don't allow your intense need to achieve lead you to loneliness.

Good relationships are just as vital to your life as your physical and mental condition. How many people can you count who you were extremely close to but suddenly, one day, the flame was gone. Daily calls became birthday calls and awkward pauses. At some point, the two of you stopped tending the garden of your friendship. The weeds grew too tall. Think of your current friends or close kin and ask yourself who's next to go? Which relationships have you neglected and used your hectic schedule as a defense for your absence.

In the end, you won't remember how many hours you studied. Your clients won't come visit you when you are sick or lose a family member. Only true, intimate relationships will sail. All others will sink.

Challenge

Write up a list of the people in your life who you couldn't bear to lose. Make a schedule and keep track of when you last spoke with them.

How often would you need to communicate in order to keep the ties strong? Make an effort to look at the list every day and track your interactions.

This is extra work. Certainly, but isn't this work worth doing to keep your friendship or partnership or marriage? I know it is. This path, this sidewalk, to peace is not for the moment but for the long run.

Soul Talk

I will water my relationships today.
I will place deep connections at the top of my priority list and experience a life of lasting fulfillment.

30

The Chess Moves

*"You need a strategy for when
the inevitable happens."*

— love collins

The citywide chess tournament had begun. Students from every age group were at the public library sitting quietly and staring at chessboards covered in black and white pieces. Hours later, two boys sat down at a long, rectangular table. One was a sixth grader; the other was a seventh grader. At the start of the championship round for their age group, the sixth grader was certain he would win since he had finally gotten good enough to beat his father at their evening chess matches.

He moved his first pawn one space forward. The boy across from him did the same thing. Being careful, the sixth grader moved another pawn, this time two spaces ahead. The seventh grader smiled and slid his queen directly in line with the sixth grader's exposed king. His heart sank to his toes. "Check mate."

The sixth grader fell for the first trick in the book: Fool's Mate. He lost that day because the wiser seventh grader went in with a strategy, and he did not. Likewise, you know even before your day starts that something is eventually going to try to capture and immobilize your positive energy. I don't care how upbeat you are, nobody is enthused 100 percent of the time. You need a strategy for when the inevitable happens. What moves do you make to keep from falling for life's Fool's Mate?

Challenge

Apply the 3M strategy: movement, motivation and music.

Movement enhances your mood. Psychologically, there is a link between the way you feel and what you do physically. Yes, you must be still in order to enter a place of peace, but there's a difference between stillness and sulkiness. When you're in a negative space, the best strategy is to get moving. Walk or run for a few minutes. Dance. Hit a punching bag (not a person). The goal is to activate your nervous system because movement impacts your mood.

Motivation breeds motivation. Whatever we wish to receive most, we must give the most. The best strategy for motivating yourself is to motivate others. When you send a motivational quote to a friend or post an encouraging thought on social media, you sharpen your own sword. Any teacher will tell you that the best way to learn something is to explain the concept to another person. When you motivate others, you internalize the message. In exchange, you are empowered.

Music changes your mode. Actually, the term *mode* in music refers to a scale or rhythmic scheme. Imagine you are a jukebox. People feed you their penny opinions and problems, and then you start to sing the same sad songs. You can change your internal song through the vibrations of music. Gather a playlist of your favorite tracks and listen to them when you feel yourself sinking into the wrong mode. Include happy, upbeat tracks that will lift you to a higher emotional altitude. It works. That's the power of music; it changes your mode.

Soul Talk

Never again will I enter the day without a strategy. I will be ready for any opposition. I will move. I will motivate others. I will use music to change my mode.

31

Be Humble

"Humility is not thinking less of yourself,
it is thinking of yourself less."
— C.S. Lewis

Pride is a cancer. Humility is the cure. Your fierce need to be seen, to be heard, to be right all the time is symptomatic of an infected ego. The word humility is a descendant of the Latin word *humilis*, meaning *low*, but humility is not about devaluating yourself. It's about valuing others. When you finally escape your own bubble, you notice that the world is equally weighed down with its own concerns. You are not alone. You can be at peace.

You don't have to win or even fight every battle. A humble person understands that being right is not always a victory. Instead of trying to make people believe exactly what you believe, sometimes it's better just to hold your tongue.

My pastor, Rev. Robert L. Johnson, told this story to the congregation one Sunday: You're at a stoplight at a four-way intersection. Your light is red. The other cars are speeding by. Their stoplight is turning yellow. They're still zooming past. Your foot is easing off the breaks because you know your light is about to turn green as soon as theirs goes red. Instead of applying their breaks, the cars in front of you break the law and continue speeding. Question: Would you be legally right to drive now that your light is green?

Of course you would. You would also be dead right. How many relationships have crashed because someone was too prideful to give the other person a pass. You would enjoy so much more peace if you would only allow others to have the right of way sometimes.

Humble yourself enough to overlook people's tendency to be human. Humble yourself enough to listen. Humble yourself enough to sacrifice your ego and consider the other perspective. Get low. A soldier in the heat of battle keeps her head down as the bullets fly past, and she remains alive. Diamonds are formed low in the Earth's mantle. Everyone knows that if his or her clothes catch fire to *stop, drop (get low), and roll.*

There is value in humility. You can spot arrogance a month away. Arrogant and prideful people treat others as if they are not worthy. This repels love, friendship, and ultimately happiness.

Challenge

Practice treating everyone you meet as if they are the most important person in the world. Give them your full attention. Make them know how special they truly are to you.

People will treat you as special in return because genuine humility is so rare. Sadly, we are not accustomed to loving-kindness. Most people are humble only toward individuals who they feel have some kind of authority over them or who they can get something from. There is no soul above your soul.

Be humble because you are connected with everyone. The same air they breathe out, you breathe in. They contain a piece of you. They too depend on the soul food of love to survive.

Soul Talk

I am humble.
I don't mind getting low because I have walked through valleys and mountains.
I treat them the same. I don't mind losing sometimes because some battles are not worth my energy. I recognize that it takes true strength to be humble. I am strong.

32

The Motto

"It's all good."

Three nights and two days had passed. A woman called me in a panic. She and our mutual friend were supposed to meet up over the weekend. "I think something could be wrong," she said, her voice trembling a little. "He hasn't responded to my texts, and his phone went straight to voicemail." We agreed to go check on him. She picked me up. On the car ride to his apartment I could tell her mind was conjuring up worst-case scenarios. Finally, we parked and took the elevator to his floor. Three knocks and two deep breaths later he came to the door confused. "Is everything alright?" I asked.

"Yeah, it's all good."

It usually is. What are you worried about today? Moving to a new city, taking a big exam, starting a job or business, speaking before a crowd, or beginning a new relationship are all exciting. They can also feel terrifying. There's so much uncertainty. "Will I succeed?" "Will they like me?" The amount of information you don't know and the lingering questions can overwhelm you.

If you dig to the root of your anxiety, you will find sprouts of fear. Your imagination is getting the best of you again. All the bad you think could happen probably never will. It's all good.

A better question is what is the *best-case scenario*? You might make a dozen new friends. You might ace the exam. The boss might love you. Your employees might love you. The crowd might love you. Your new romantic partner might love you. It takes the same mental effort to think of the worst as it does to imagine the best alternative.

There's no benefit or wisdom in lying in your bed the night before your big day scared of what might happen. In this moment, there is no real danger. Give yourself permission to be free. Eat breakfast. If you're going to lose your appetite, at least wait until the scary thing actually shows up. Otherwise, you'll spend the day torturing yourself and running from a shadow that never shows.

Challenge

Next time you start listing woeful *what ifs,* remind yourself that it's all good. Take your fear to its logical conclusion. Let's say you actually do bomb the test or the person doesn't end up liking you or the business tanks. Then what?

You bounce back. Period.

You study harder the next semester. You open up to new opportunities, and start dating again. You find someone who respects and accepts you for who you are. No matter what: it's all good. You simply keep going forward until you win again. You embrace your true identity: more than a conqueror.

Soul Talk

It's all good.

I will use my imagination constructively in moments of uncertainty.

I will expect the best and I will receive the best today.

33

The Emancipation

*Your chains have been
begging you to let them go.*
— love collins

Free yourself. Whenever a person holds desperately to things or people or circumstances, it is a sign of inner insecurity. It indicates a fear of loss. We tend to enslave the things we are afraid will run away, but fear does not cohabit with peace. The place of liberty is the place of surrender.

Think of the giant trees in California's Sequoia and King Canyon National Park. One of the largest ones there, the General Sherman, stands 274 feet tall. It has lived for nearly two millenniums. In the year 1978, a massive branch bigger than most trees broke off, but the fall did not harm the General Sherman. Still and steady, it kept standing.[ii]

Could it be that this is also the way to achieve a more lasting peace? When you become less attached to the fleeting branches and more attached to the essential trunk of life, one fallen branch or a few tumbling leaves cannot shake you to your core and uprooted you.

Sure you want to be accepted and loved by others, but at what cost? It's so easy to hitch your self-esteem to the back of how many likes you get on social media or how much money you have in the bank. These things are fickle. You can be loved today and hated tomorrow. Detach from the things that exist outside of your essential self. You are not the grades you make in school or the position you hold. You are not even your body. You are the soul underneath. All other things are outer garments, shadows, and echoes of your true self.

Your chains have been begging you to let them go. Cling to your soul. Let all else fall to the ground. Being detached from outer things does not mean despising or hating them; it simply means not needing them. Rather than needing to be accepted, you are free to focus on accepting others. Instead of seeking attention, you seek opportunities to be attentive. You give people permission to be who they are and let them hold the views they hold. You relinquish control of every detail of your life and make room for unexpected to happen.

How? How do you simply let go? One way is to abandon the idea that you can save the world. All you can do is love it. That's the greatest command. The world needs more compassion than correction.

The Sequoia has endured so many years because it doesn't allow itself to be uprooted just because a single branch falls. Take its advice and don't be shaken when a plan doesn't work out or a financial situation becomes unstable. Hold on to the essential and let all else go.

Soul Talk

Today I am letting go.
Today I am letting go.
Today.

34

Balance

*"The only time a juggler
appeals to me
is when I see him
miss the ball."*
— Khalil Gibran

How do you do it? How do you juggle all the responsibilities and expectations tossed at you from others while walking across the balancing beam of your own life?

Some days it's easy, but most days it can feel as if there's a brick tied to your ankle and you keep flailing your arms just to stay steady. So many things demand time and attention: your relationships, your personal health, school, your job, and not to mention your own dreams that tug at your sleeve constantly. You are only one person with two hands and twenty-four hours, but there is a way.

Science calls it *ecosystem equilibrium*. An ecosystem, a community of organisms living in a particular environment, is in equilibrium when all the species have stable population sizes. Take squirrels, for instance. Let's say one summer the number of squirrels in your city increases dramatically. Meanwhile, the supply of acorns stays the same. They all eat the nuts that fall from the same trees yet since there are so many squirrels, there's not enough food to go around. Tragically, some of them starve.

Fast-forward a year. Because some didn't make it, your city now has fewer squirrels this season, which means more acorns for those who live there. This time all of the squirrels survive. Nature returns to her balanced state. So what does it take for your internal ecosystem to do the same?

Number one: balance is never instantaneous.

It took time for chaos to find you; it takes time for you to find peace. Balance is not a few minutes of serenity but a way of life. The reason this book includes daily practices for peace and positivity is because no single technique can create lasting results. If you want your soul to mature, it takes persistent practice in all areas of your life.

Number two: everything is interrelated.

What affects the oak tree, affects the squirrel. It makes no difference that your body is fit and tone if your relationships are sagging and your dreams are lagging. Giving a third of your energy to your career, a third to your relationships, and a third to your education often leaves all of them undernourished. Prioritize and decide what deserves more of your time. What you value most is easily determined by asking yourself: "What and who could I not do without?" Give them what is due. When you give of yourself, give 100 percent. Balance is not about equality; it's about equity. Rather than distributing equal time to each area, give each what it deserves.

Number three: some things must go.

Demand can get so high that you have to scratch one or two priorities from your list altogether. Don't expect it to be painless. Nobody wants to see a squirrel go hungry, but certain habits are unsustainable. Running from place to place out of breath and drained by the time you finally make it home is not healthy long-term. Remove what cannot stay and allocate that space to your most precious priorities.

Soul Talk

Balance may be slow to achieve, but I am willing to smile while I wait. Today I will give the most important things the most of me.

35

The No-Media Diet

*"Technology is a useful servant
but a dangerous master."*
— Christian Lous Lange

Media is like a triple-layer chocolate cake. You can only consume so much in one period of time. The benefit of going on a diet or even a fast is the shift it causes in your body. It gives your stomach a break from the heavy lifting it normally does. You don't realize how weighty and full you are until you experience the lightness in your legs after a few days with less food.

You ingest media daily. Like a dessert, media tastes good to you, but it's not always good for you. For years, I would wake up every morning and watch the news. My eyes soaked up all of the dreadful things that were transpiring in the world while my mouth inhaled a bowl of cereal. Eventually, I began to notice how jaded I felt after viewing the bad news day after day. I changed my media diet. I sold my TV on eBay.

Replace your morning news with some inspiring music or an inspirational video. You don't have to sell your TV, but it is important to step away. The world's problems will still be there after breakfast. Plus, there's little you can do by staring at them on a screen. The overload of negative news can increase cortisol levels in your body, which activates stress. Notice how light your mind feels and how productive you are after a few days away from the tube.

At times, though, the TV is not the issue. It's social media. You might need a Facebook fast. Social media is useful because it keeps us all connected and informed, but it can quickly drive many of us into the comparison game. You start to measure your life by the virtual appearance of someone else's life. You see a friend getting engaged, having a baby, or traveling and then feelings of envy and even inadequacy begin to simmer inside.

You can quickly become a volcano of emotion. We open ourselves to the judgment of others. Every picture posted and each status scribed comes with an instant mark of approval or criticism. Thumbs and hearts become obsessions and addictions.

Challenge

Go on a no-media diet. If you find it too challenging to stay off social media for a few days, try a few hours. If you're still tempted, power off your phone or computer.

As you begin to realize that you can go without media and constant stimulation, your appetite for them will diminish. You will be free to think fresh ideas and get long overdue chores done. That is it's own reward. Freedom from judging and being judged will reset your happiness. Once your diet or fast is complete, the new, healthier habits will have moved in.

Soul Talk

Today I will shun bad news and seek good news. I will develop a healthy media diet and lifestyle.

36

The Natural State

*"I went to the woods because
I wished to live deliberately."*
— Henry David Thoreau

Walk into the forest. Climb to the top of a mountain. Dive into a pool. Notice how true it feels. It's like returning home; it's so familiar.

We are made of nature. The natural state within each of us is serene and peaceful. Much of our frustration comes from being so distant from our truest environment. You're not upset, you're home sick. When you lose connection with nature, you lose connection with yourself. No wonder we call her *mother*.

The wind in your chest brings you oxygen. The sun on your skin keeps you warm. At least three-fourths of you is water. The same water on earth today has been here forever. There is no new water. It merely cycles from the ocean to the clouds and back again—evaporation and precipitation.

Thus, you are at once young and ancient because the pieces of you are old. We seem to forget that we are connected with all that is. We are trees with feet. We are mountains that move. We carry droplets of the ocean inside these cups of flesh.

What does all this mean? It means you should grab a calculator. Add up the hours you spend inside inhaling filtered air? How much time do you sit at a desk, a seat, bending your body in a position it was never meant to bend. Do you remember what the sun feels like? How many artificial sounds have your ears heard today? How many clicks, cash registers, alarm clocks or car horns have you encountered?

These experiences are unavoidable. They are part of modern life, but you've got to escape every now and then. A ten-minute walk through the park or down the street can bring you back to the present moment.

Challenge

Pick up a leaf. Notice how fragile it is, like your life. Grab a rock. Feel how enduring and strong it seems. Thousands of small pieces of sediment have gathered together in your palm for just a moment.

You too are a gathering of atoms and molecules. This connection with nature reminds you that you are not separate. You are part of a larger, magnificent creation. This knowledge is liberating because it is truth. Holy Scripture says, "You shall know the truth and the truth shall make you free." Open yourself to the freedom that comes with knowing you are not alone. You are a part of nature. The more you encounter nature the more harmonious you will become.

Soul Talk

I am one of nature's many miracles.
I feel connected when I return to my first home.
Today I will practice periods of communing with nature.

37

Remember this

"This above all: to thine own self be true…"
— William Shakespeare

Know you. Remember that scene in *The Lion King* where Mufasa appeared in the sky and reminded Simba that he was royalty? Simba was feeling depressed and dejected. He had forgotten that he was meant to be a king. Uncle Scar had convinced Simba as a cub that he was the reason for his father's death. He believed the false narrative of himself and accepted the idea that he was unworthy.

It's easy for us to forget who we are. Have you forgotten your royal heritage? You are more than what your current condition gives you credit for. You are not your location: in the dirt, yet a diamond; in poverty, yet containing riches; in the midst of criticism, but self-assured. Never make the mistake of confusing what *you're in* with what's *in you.*

You belong to the same species as Shakespeare, Alexander the Great, Jesus, Mother Teresa, and Ghandi. If you find yourself feeling the weight of inadequacy, remember your humanness is just as human as theirs. "I come as one; I stand as ten thousand," wrote Maya Angelou. Within you is not just a queen or king but kingdoms. Therefore, you are too regal for negativity. You need not be in panic because peace must appear at your command. This too is just a narrative. It only crystalizes into belief when you cast constant anchors in your mind to activate your faith.

Challenge

On your bathroom mirror, on your bedroom wall, on the desk in your office, and on the background of our cellphone, place truth triggers.

Truth triggers are simple, subtle messages that usher into your mind the thoughts of who you truly desire to be. They banish those thoughts that depict the false identity you or others have painted.

One weekend, a group of my roommate's friends came over to visit our apartment. A girl looked at his bedroom door and then looked at mine. "Why does your say 'A+'?" she asked. I told her I didn't want to keep seeing the letter B. The apartment owners had labeled each door A and B to distinguish the rooms for rent purposes. I covered up the B because I didn't want to receive the subliminal message of "average" every time I entered my sanctuary. I wanted to walk into an A+ room and, ultimately, an A+ life.

It may seem trivial, but the small things compound and make the biggest difference. Give attention to the details in your life. What radio station is your radio turned to when you first enter your vehicle? What images of inspiration are on your computer screen? It matters. Everything matters.

Eventually the way you define yourself becomes implicit memory. Deep groves are dug into your psyche over the years. If you are not careful, sand can get tossed over the truth and cover the memory of who you really are.

Soul Talk

I know who I am.
I am a person of peace.
I am a person of love.
I am phenomenal.
I enter as a drop, but my presence is the ocean.

38

The Reason I'm M.A.D.

"Self," I whispered,
"Let's make a decision."
— love collins

Who are you going to be—victim or victor? How are you going to be—powerful or powerless? You soul is a lion roaring. It will not be still until you confront yourself and the fact that you have been bound by indecision. If there is a small uneasiness you feel from day to day that has not ceased, it is because you have yet to fully make a decision.

We have all felt it—that clawing, gnawing feeling that something has been left undone which must be completed. That something is you. No matter how successful you are, one fact is undisputed: you are not all of who you can be. At some point, you're going to have to get mad. Fall out with mediocrity. Get mad at stagnation. Get mad because you've been standing in a dark room full of potential when there is a light switch right beside you. Today is the day to make a decision.

"It takes more courage to examine the dark corners of your own soul than it does for a soldier to fight on a battlefield," said Walter B. Yeats. Have ever you truly examined yourself? Have you looked intently at the broken pieces of your character?

This week, hopefully, you brushed your teeth. You made a decision that it would not be appropriate to speak to people with bad breath or food stuck between your molars. You probably brushed them more than once. The decision was easy. You've made the same decision so many times that it's now so engrained in your subconscious that it is more of a reflex than a choice. It is a part of your habit orbit. Your habit orbit is controlled by the decisions you make and fail to make on a regular basis. Every semester during finals, without fail, my face would break out. I would get so nervous while studying or during a test that I would scratch it and irritate my skin.

One day I had to remind myself: "You have taken hundreds of test, and none of them have killed you. Find joy in the opportunity to get an education. You have stuck to your diet for months, surely you can overcome this." Talk to yourself. I made a decision not to allow myself to be controlled. I reinforced my decision over and over by reminding myself of the commitment and rehearsing scriptures and quotes on freedom and self-control. What happened next was a paradigm shift, my habit orbit began to switch. Remind yourself of a decision you made in the past and committed to. You will be able to summon the strength of that occasion and transmute it to any obstacle you are facing.

Challenge

If you have never made a long-term decision and stuck to it, make a decision now to re-read a chapter of this book (or any book) every day at the same time for the next week to build your commitment muscle.

No wonder the third step of the Alcoholics Anonymous' Twelve-Step program begins with the words "Make a decision." The path of liberation and peace demands decision.

Soul Talk

I am M.A.D. today. I am making a decision.
I will be who I could have been and do what I should have done. I commit.

39

The Love Letter

"Every act rewards itself. "
— Ralph Waldo Emerson

Give nothing permission to drown you. These are strange times. There's so much anger and so much division. The waves of hate keep raging, but you must not surrender to them. Turn the bow of your ship toward lovelier waters.

Newspapers and newsfeeds are full of people offending and taking offense. The option to exchange evil for evil is evergreen. You could choose to retaliate. The issue with retaliation, as justified as it may seem, is that it triggers a powerful law: The Law of Compensation. "Whatsoever a man soweth, that shall he also reap," reads Scripture.

Sow love; reap love. Sow a slap; reap a fist. Plant seeds of selfishness and reap a harvest of resentfulness. Call it payback. Call it Karma. There is no escaping the truth that what goes around comes back around. Life will compensate you for whatever you do, so do good and love. To love is to serve. Ask the world: "How may I serve today?"

It will repay you in abundance. Every time you encounter another human being, look to serve them by offering them something: money, a compliment, a piece of candy, some positive feedback, anything. Even if you only have time to give them a smile, offer it as if it is golden charm.

Think about the individual whose personality you most admire. Aren't they friendly? Don't they smile and laugh? People give them so much attention. That's because they give others attention. Give someone the affection you desire today. Send a quick text, a kind thought, or even a prayer. So often our prayers tend to go no further than our own ceilings because they are self-absorbed petitions. To pray for others is to say: "God, it's OK. I'm so thankful for my many blessings that I want to see you bless others as well."

Why limit your love to people? Send love to all: to the air that finds its home inside of your lungs, to the birds who sing their songs to you, to the clouds who send rain. Send love to your food as you cook it or to the person you are witnessing prepare it for you.

Send love to your wallet and your bank account and the parts of you that you may dislike. Send a string-less love, looking for nothing in return. Be so filled that you overflow to the point where love is all you have to give.

Challenge

Every time you have a conversation with someone, silently think to them: "I love you as myself." They will not hear your secret, but they will know you have one by the warmth of your cheeks and the way your eyes meet their eyes. They will feel the love even though they can't see it. Do this even for those people you dislike, especially for those people.

And why should you? They need it most. There is a grain of good and a drop of you in them. There is something in everyone worth loving.

Soul Talk

I will send love all day today.
My eyes will peer with beauty and joy on every-
thing before them.
Beauty, joy, love I shall receive.

40

Be

You are a human being. Be.
— love collins

Be here. Come with me onto the pages of a brown, leather-bound notebook. Blackbirds outside my slightly cracked window are flying from tree to tree chirping. Their feathers are wet. It has just rained. The leaves on the soft ground are soggy, and my dog Missy is in the backyard sleeping.

This is what it means to *be here.* Teach your soul to be exactly where you are in each moment. Name what you see around you as a child does while playing *I spy.* Be fully present in mind and body in every space you occupy until peace occupies you.

Chances are you learned to write English in first grade. Remember how you were so excited, and a little nervous, on your first day of school. When you got to class and sat down, the teacher told you: "Do well this year, and one day you will make it to second grade. You did well. The dominoes fell and kept falling. You went from anticipating elementary school to dreaming of junior high. In high school you couldn't wait to go to college or enter the workforce or fight for your country. The cycle continued.

The final destination, however, never arrives. There's always another degree, another position or another certification to reach for. You find yourself never stopping to really enjoy *this moment.* Just be for once. Being conscious of where you are without giving excessive attention to the future is liberating. "Who will I marry? When will I graduate? What city will I live in? How will I make enough money?" These are all questions worth asking but to linger on them is to sacrifice present peace for future uncertainty.

One of our basic human needs is assurance. We all know tomorrow is out of our hands but that doesn't stop us from thinking about it and planning compulsively for it. All the planning gives us a false sense of power over our lives. Don't let fantasizing about tomorrow make you miss today. Try to taste each moment. Savor it as if it is your last.

Challenge

Take a shower tonight. See if you can trace the water as it flows. Notice how it hits your neck, trickles down the small of your back then over your thigh and finally grazes your toenail.

Take time today to observe yourself. What or who are you forgetting? How sternly or kindly are you speaking? Are your lips too tight? Can you soften your face and lower your shoulders a little?

You are a human being. Be. Contrary to what everyone else may say, your primary human vocation is not to do; it is to be. Be here. Be still. Be free from disease. That's right: dis-ease. Constantly trying to be elsewhere is an illness. It means you are uneasy with being *here*. Get comfortable within your own skull and skin.

As my barber would always tell me on my way out of his one-room barbershop, "Be easy."

Soul Talk

Be easy, my soul.

ABOUT THE AUTHOR

Love Collins is the pen name of KenDrell D. Collins.
Collins studies law at the University of Arkansas
School of Law, but he also studies people. He has lived
among the easy-goers of southern Texas, the siesta-
takers of Spain, the fast-movers of the District of
Columbia, and the go-getters of New York City.
Everywhere he has traveled, the people search for
peace. Be Steady, My Soul is a collection of practical
lessons designed for slow, daily application. This book
is by no means the destination of peace and positivity,
but it is a map.

email: lovecollinsbooks@gmail.com

love collins

[i] *The Story-Life of Lincoln* by Wayne Whipple. The JC Winston Co, 1908. pp. 481-482.

[ii] *General Sherman Tree Facts* by Joanne Thomas. USA Today. http://traveltips.usatoday.com/general-sherman-tree-61028.html.

Made in the USA
Coppell, TX
02 September 2020

35621398R00075